# It's Alright to Write

# It's Alright to Write

Joseph Edward Lohman

Copyright © 2010 by Joseph Edward Lohman.

| Library of Congress Control Number: | | 2010906095 |
|---|---|---|
| ISBN: | Hardcover | 978-1-4500-9184-8 |
| | Softcover | 978-1-4500-9183-1 |
| | Ebook | 978-1-4500-9185-5 |

All rights reserved. No part of this book may be reproduced or transmitted in any form or by any means, electronic or mechanical, including photocopying, recording, or by any information storage and retrieval system, without permission in writing from the copyright owner.

This book was printed in the United States of America.

**To order additional copies of this book, contact:**
Xlibris Corporation
1-888-795-4274
www.Xlibris.com
Orders@Xlibris.com

# CONTENTS

But What Awaits for Life ...................................................... 7
A Marine ................................................................................ 9
When Love is All that Matters .......................................... 15
This is Our History ............................................................ 17
The Life of a Marine ......................................................... 20
My Greatest Defeat ........................................................... 22
When Life's Experiences . . . ............................................ 24
The House of which My Foundation is Built On .......... 26
His Noise ............................................................................ 27
This Life ............................................................................. 29
Again .................................................................................. 31
Your Childrens Plan ......................................................... 32
I Hoped They'd Say I Made a Difference ...................... 33
Distress .............................................................................. 34
What's Next ...................................................................... 36
The Stitching Stare ........................................................... 38
War / Art / Train / Inside / Wartrainside ...................... 39
Home is not Really a Place at All .................................... 40
Is it Inspiration ................................................................. 42
The Limits of Image ......................................................... 43
A Primitive GivIng ........................................................... 44
J. O. Y. ............................................................................... 45
Just a Smile ....................................................................... 47
A Farmers Hardship ........................................................ 48
silence in my room .......................................................... 49
my lady .............................................................................. 50
Julianne & Joseph ............................................................ 51

## BUT WHAT AWAITS FOR LIFE

AS I'VE GONE THROUGH A FOURTH OF MY YEARS—THERE'S BEEN SAD TIMES, GOOD TIMES, LAUGHS, AND TEARS—THERE'S BEEN GREAT MEMORIES AND SOME I'D RATHER NOT REMEMBER—BUT MY FAITH IN THE LORD IS WHAT KEEPS ME STRONG AND HOLDS ME TOGETHER—I'VE LOVED AND I'VE LOST—I'VE GIVEN IN AND I'VE HELD BACK—BUT I'VE ALWAYS STOOD TALL—AND I THANK MY PARENTS FOR THAT—I'VE OPENED DOORS AND OTHERS—I'VE LOCKED AWAY—BUT I ALWAYS LOOK FORWARD TO THE NEXT DAY—NOW THE LORD GIVES ME THE STRENGTH FOR EACH DAY—HE HAS BLESSED ME WITH A GOOD HEART AND A GOOD FAMILY—TO WHICH IS WHY I'M HERE TODAY—THE UNITED STATES MARINE CORPS—THEIR SAFETY IS MY # 1 CONCERN AND I STAND BESIDE MY BROTHERS AND SISTERS TO ENSURE THAT—THOUGH IN THESE TIMES—YES, IT IS TOUGH, IT'S TOUGH FOR NOT JUST THE MARINES TRAINING FOR WAR—IT'S TOUGH FOR THE MOM THAT RECIEVES THE NEWS THAT HER SON IS NOT COMING HOME ANYMORE—FOR HOW DO YOU TELL THE REST OF THE FAMILY THAT YOUR BROTHER OR YOUR SON WON'T BE BACK—THE TEARS BUILD UP BUT CAN'T BE HELD BACK—BECAUSE THAT MARINE MAY NOT HAVE BEEN JUST A BROTHER OR A SON BUT PERHAPS A HUSBAND OR EVEN WORSE A FATHER—NOW LEAVING HIS CHILD TO GROW UP AND WONDER—THAT'S NOT A LIFE FOR ANYONE TO SIT AND PONDER—BUT AS THE STORY UNFOLDS—LIFE WILL GO ON FOR THE BETTER—THOUGH SOME—MAY NOT WANT TO HEAR THOSE WORDS—BUT REALIZE HE GAVE HIS LIFE, NOT JUST FOR HIS COUNTRY BUT FOR OTHERS TO PROSPER—FOR NOW HE IS NEXT TO THE LORD—HIS FAITH LED HIM TO BE THE MAN KNOWN TO ALL AS NOT JUST A HERO OR A

GOOD PERSON, BUT A MARINE—
FOR EVERYONE KNOWS—US, MARINES, WE
COME WITH THE UPMOST RESPECT,—HONOR, COURAGE,
AND COMMITMENT. THOSE ARE OUR CORE VALUES
WE LIVE IT AND WE BREATH IT AND EVERYDAY
WE SHOW IT—SO NEXT TIME YOU SEE A MARINE
THINK OF THIS LETTER AND KNOW THE SACRIFICES
WE MAKE—

*20090303*

## A MARINE

TIMES ARE TOUGH IN TIMES OF WAR—
BUT THE GLORY OF VICTORY COMES
WITH A PRICE OF GORE—
AS THE DEATH
COUNT RISES—THE FREEDOM BIRTH—
OF ANOTHER AMERICAN—ONLY RISES
THE GIFT OF LIFE IS GIVEN AND IT'S
ALSO TAKEN—SO AT THIS HOUR
WE THANK GOD FOR HIS CREATION—
AND WE GIVE THANKS TO EACH TOWER—
BY WHICH—WERE TAKEN ON 9-11—
BUT REVENGE OR WHAT YOU CALL IT—
MUST HAPPEN—SOMETHING MUST BE
DONE—JUST LIKE VIETNAM, KOREA,
WWII AND WWI—THE FIRE IN MY
EYES—THE HATRED IN MY HEART—THE
GUN IN MY HAND—AS A MARINE—
I WILL BE THE 1ST TO STAND—THE
POWER OF THE PEOPLE ARE GREATER EVEN,
THAN THIS LAND—MY FOREFATHERS WROTE OF
LIFE, LIBERTY, AND THE PURSUIT OF HAPPINESS—
STATEMENTS OF INSTITUTIONS—THAT CAN'T
BE BROKEN—CAN'T BE BENT—NOT EVEN
SLIGHTLY—BECAUSE WEAKNESS IS NOT A PART OF OUR
FORTITUDE—THERE IS NO OTHER TYPE OF ATTITUDE—
SO THIS IS OUR GRATITUDE—AND AS A MARINE,
SOMETIMES YOU MUST WITHHOLD THE TRUTH BUT
FOR THE MOST PART—WE ARE HONORABLE, TRUSTWORTHY,
CONSIDERABLE, RESPECTFUL AND MOST OF ALL—
YOUR 1ST CALL—ONE OTHER THING—
RULES AND THE BIGGEST LAWS SOMETIMES
NEED TO BE BROKEN—IT'S WHAT OUR COUNTRY
STANDS ON—TO FIX THE PROBLEM YOU MUST
HAVE A SOLUTION—AND OUR 13 COLONIES DID A
DAMN FINE JOB OF WRITING THE CONSTITUTION—

*9/12/08*

I HAVE SEEN MANY OF
SUNSETS JUST AS THE
ONE TONIGHT—BUT NOT
ONE IS THE EXACT SAME-
PERHAPS IT IS A MINUTE
OFF FROM THE NIGHT
BEFORE—A LEAF HAS FALLEN
FROM A TREE THAT WAS
ONCE FULL OF LIFE—A
ROCK HAS BEEN THROWN
AND NOW SITS IN A
DIFFERENT SPOT—THE
WIND BLOWS COLDER THAN
THE WEEK BEFORE AND YET
IT IS THE SAME—OR PERHAPS
IT IS A MINUTE EARLIER
THAN THE NIGHT BEFORE—A
LEAF STILL STRETCHES FROM
THE TREE THAT IS FULL OF LIFE—
A ROCK THAT HAS SAT IN THE
SAME SPOT SINCE TIME BEGAN—
THE WIND, WHICH IS OF NONE, IS
AS STILL AS THE MOMENT WE ARE
IN—AND YET IT IS THE SAME—

*Sat. July 11th 2009*

LET THE WORLD SEE THERE ARE GOOD MEN—
WHEN EVER YOUR LAST SUNSET COMES—
MAY YOU KNOW THAT YOUR LIFE WAS LIVED GOOD—
MAY YOUR FAMILY BE PROUD TO SAY THAT'S MY BROTHER—
OR YOUR PARENTS PROUD TO SAY THAT THAT'S MY SON—
OR YOUR GIRLFRIEND PROUD TO SAY, THAT'S MY BOYFRIEND—
OR YOUR KIDS PROUD TO SAY, THAT'S MY DADDY—
OR THE ONE WE HOLD DEAR, PROUD TO SAY,
THAT'S MY HUSBAND—
MAY THEY CRY WITH JOY THAT YOU ARE WITH THE LORD—
MAY YOUR NAME BE LIVED ON, AS A HERO WHO FOUGHT—
MAY HISTORY BOOKS RECORD YOUR NAME—NOT WITH FAME
OR FORTUNE—NOT WITH BEING THE POORIEST
OR THE ROUGHEST—
BUT BEING THAT LIGHT TO LEAD HIS SUBORDINATES
INTO BATTLE—
BEING THE FIRST ONE TO STEP OFF AND THE
LAST ONE TO STEP ON—
BEING THE PEACEMAKER RATHER THAN THE BRUTAL
MURDERER—
BEING THAT MIRACLE FOR THE SICK RATHER THAN
THE POISEN FOR THE RICH
LET THE WORLD SEE THERE ARE GOOD MEN—
MAY YOUR SQUAD BE PROUD TO SAY, THAT'S MY BROTHER—
MAY YOUR PLATOON BE PROUD TO SAY, THAT'S MY BROTHER—
MAY YOUR COMPANY BE PROUD TO SAY, THAT'S MY BROTHER—
OUR BROTHER WAS ONLY A PRIVATE—BUT IN OUR EYES—
HE WAS HIGHER RANKED THAN A COLONEL.—HIS
CHARACTER—WAS A BLESSING
HIS ENTHUISIASM FOR HELPING OTHERS—WAS A BLESSING—
HIS GIFT OF GIVING—WAS A BLESSING—
LET THE WORLD SEE THERE ARE GOOD MEN—
OUR BROTHER—KNEW THE COST THAT FREEDOM
WOULD COST—
OUR SON—KNEW THE DANGERS
MY BOYFRIEND—SAID HE WANTED TO DEFEND—

MY DADDY—SAID HE WOULD BE BACK SOON—
MY LOVE AND JOY—TOLD ME IF HE DOESN'T MAKE IT BACK—
THAT HE WILL SEE ME SOON—
LET THE WORLD SEE THERE ARE GOOD MEN—

*20090727*

## WHEN Love is all that MAtTers

LOVE
IS NOT ALWAYS . . .
IT'S NOT ALWAYS EASY
IT'S NOT ALWAYS PLEASANT
SOMETIMES YOU MIGHT ARGUE
AND SOMETIMES YOU MIGHT
    LUST
THERE ARE TEMPTATIONS
FAR MORE—BUT THAT'S
WHERE THE DIVINE LOVE
HOLDS UP—IT'S WHEN LOVE
IS TESTED OVER AND OVER
AND STILL CONTINUES TO
GROW—NOW EVEN THOUGH
EACH DAY AS YOU GET
UP MIGHT SEEM THE
SAME—IT IS NOT—FOR
LOVE WILL BRING TRIALS
AND TRIBULATIONS, HURTFUL
MOMENTS, AND
    DISHEARTENING
MOMENTS BUT THROUGH ALL
OF THE CHAOS MAY YOU
COME TO FIND THAT LOVE
IS ALWAYS . . .
IT'S ALWAYS PROMISING
IT'S ALWAYS EVERLASTING
SOMETIMES YOU WILL HOLD
ONTO IT AND SOMETIMES
IT WILL HOLD ONTO YOU—
THERE IS NO GREATER
THING THAT WE
WILL FIND, BUT IN
LIFE—IT'S SOMETIMES—ALL
WE NEED TO GET US
THROUGH THIS TIME—
BUT AFTER THE ROUGH
PATCH IN THE ROAD—
NEVER LOSE SIGHT OF
THE GOOD THINGS YOU
    HAVE—
HOLD ONTO THEM AND
THEY WILL HOLD
ONTO YOU—TRUST IN
THEM AND THEY WILL
TRUST IN YOU AND MOST
OF ALL Love them
AND THEY WILL LOVE YOU—
JULIANNE, I WANT YOU TO
KNOW THAT I LOVE YOU

*DEC 6<sup>TH</sup> 2007*

## THIS IS OUR HISTORY

WHEN THE DAYS SUNSET DRAWS NEAR
OUR ENEMY'S MIND FILLS WITH FEAR—
BECAUSE THEY KNOW THE EFFECTIVENESS
OF A MARINE AT NIGHT IS A HELL
OF ALOT WORSE THAN WHEN THERE'S
LIGHT—JUST GIVE US THE NECESSITIES—
AND HEAR ABOUT HOW WE ACCOMPLISHED
OUR MISSIONS AND DID OUR DUTIES—
HONOR, COURAGE, AND COMMITMENT—
THAT'S OUR 24 HOURS A DAY
MINDSET—AND WILL BE UNTIL OUR FINAL DAY
OF JUDGEMENT—
SO THAT'S WHY WE SAY ONCE A MARINE ALWAYS
A MARINE—THIS CORPS OF OURS IS MADE UP
OF THE FEW AND THE PROUD, BUT IT'S ONLY
THESE FEW THAT REALLY GET TO KNOW THE FEELING,
REALLY EVER EXPERIENCE THE BOOK WRITTEN, HISTORY
TAUGHT, BROTHERS DYING IN EACH OTHERS ARMS, AND
LIVING WITH HIS LAST WORDS IN YOUR HEART
BUT THAT'S WHY WE NEVER FALL APART—NEVER LEAVE
A MARINE OR AN AMERICAN BEHIND—AND ALWAYS
COMPLETE OUR MISSION—NO MATTER WHAT, EVERY SINGLE
TIME

*11/23/08*

IT SEEMS THE PRESENT OF EACH DAWN—
LEAVES A FEW OF THE BEST—
AS ONE WAKES, THEIR SCHEDULE HAS
NOT SUBDUED—THEIR MIND IS STILL CLEAR
OF THE THOUGHT—THAT THIS WILL BE A
GOOD DAY—NEVER ONCE THINKING,—THAT
AWFUL THOUGHT—BUT AS YOU STRETCH
OUT—THE DOOR, CLOSE BEHIND THAT WILL
SLAME WITH A SHUTTER, YOU STOP—THAT SOUND YOU
HEAR AT THIS TIME A DAY, ONLY BRINGS
A WORRYSOME THOUGHT—AS IT RINGS
THROUGHOUT THE HOUSE—BUT THE SOUND OF
THE SHUTTER—NEVER COMES—AND THE DOOR
SWINGS BACK WIDE—ONLY TO HEAR
THE CRACK IN THE WOOD AS YOU APPROACH
THE SOUND WITH THE RING—YOUR MIND SENDS
A BREAKING COLD CHILL THROUGHOUT YOUR BODY—
AND YOUR FINGERS—THAT THIS MORNING WERE FLOWING
THROUGH THAT SOFT HAIR—NOW SKETCH A SLOW DRAGGING
FORCE ACROSS THE PHONE—AS YOU DEFY GRAVITY AND RAISE
IT TO YOUR GENTLE CHEEK—THE SOUNDS
TRANSPOSSED BRING
TEARS—THE MARINES WIFE HAS HEARD HER GREATEST FEARS—

*20090808*

# THE LIFE OF A MARINE

AT A YOUNG AGE—THEY ARE IN THE SPOTLIGHT ON STAGE—
BUT AS THEY GET OLDER—A TROUBLEMAKER—YOU START
TO PONDER—BUT AS THEY GRADUATE—THEY START TO MAKE
THEIR OWN FATE—AND THE CHOICES SOME,
ACTUALLY FEW, CHOOSE
TO TAKE—IS THAT OF A MARINE
THE COLOR THEY NOW WEAR IS GREEN—BUT THEY CAME
FROM ALL OVER, BLACK, WHITE, YOU NAME IT
AND EVERY TYPE OF
CLIMATE AND WEATHER—
THEY GO EAST OR WEST TO BEGIN THIS
NEW QUEST—IT IS THEIR BASICS—
IT IS DESIGNED TO WEED OUT
THE WEAK AND IT FORMS A BROTHERHOOD OF THE STRONG.
THEY ARE COMMITTED AND DEVOTED TO
NEVER DOING WRONG—THEIR
BY-LAWS STAND AND HAVE STOOD FOR OVER 233 YEARS—NOW
MANY WONDER HOW?, BUT IT'S ONLY THE
MOTHERS WHO FEAR—
BUT MARINES NEVER CEASE—ALTHOUGH
WE TRAIN FOR WAR—WE
PRAY FOR PEACE.—
WE ARE TRAINED TO KILL MEN—THAT'S WHY WE ARE ALL BASIC
RIFLEMAN—BUT ARE PRIMARY CONCERN—IS THAT
OF THE AMERICAN—SO
WHEN WE TRAVEL TO DISTANT LANDS—IT IS OUR GOD WE
TRUST WHO KEEPS US SAFE IN HIS HANDS—
AS WE MUST GO—WE LEAVE BEHIND FAMILY AND FRIENDS—
SOME, WE MAY COME BACK TO SEE AND SOME
WE'LL NEVER KNOW—
BUT IN OUR PATH OF TRAVEL—THE ROAD CURVES AND BENDS
ONLY TO TEACH US—THERE'S MUCH MORE TO MEND—BUT
ALL IN ALL—THERE'S ONLY ONE COUNTRY I DEFEND
FOR THE MARINE CORPS IS THE FIRST TO GET THE CALL—
IT'S NOT THAT AMERICA NEEDS US, IT'S THAT THEY WANT US
OUR VICTORY STREAK SPEAKS FOR ITSELF—WE NEVER ACCEPT
DEFEAT—JUST CHECK THE HISTORY BOOKS ON THE SHELF—

THEY DATE BACK TO WHEN HONESTY STOOD FOR WHO
YOU WERE—WHEN YOUR LAST NAME MEANT
SOMETHING, IT MEANT
EVERYTHING—AND TO THIS DAY MARINES STILL LIVE BY THOSE
READINGS—
THE LAST NAMES OF THOSE WHO GAVE THEIR
LIFE—IN ORDER TO SAVE THEIR FELLOW MARINES—THAT'S
MORE RESPECTED THAN ANY OTHER THING OUT THERE—HE
DIED FOR HIS FAMILIES FREEDOM, FOR HIS WIFE AND
KIDS AND FOR KIDS TO COME—
AMERICANS NEED TO REALIZE WHAT MARINES DO AND
WHAT THEY HAVE DONE—SO WHEN YOU SEE A MARINE
AT HOME—A THANK YOU IS ALL WE
ASK FOR—BECAUSE THE NEXT TIME YOU HEAR HIS NAME—HE
MIGHT BE WITH THE LORD—

*090510*

## MY GREATEST DEFEAT

WHEN THAT MOMENT COMES FOR EACH INDIVIDUAL—
HIS BODY HAS PAID THE PRICE—
HIS SHOULDERS FROM HIS PACK-DRIP WITH BLOOD
AND STAIN THAT GREEN SHIRT—THE SWEAT
FROM HIS BODY POURS
OUT LIKE A RIVER INTO AN OCEAN—HIS BOOTS—
TORN AND RIPPED
IN EVERY DIRECTION FROM THE TERRAIN HE HAS TRAVELED
AND YET—HE PUSHES ON—
HIS CALVES AND THIGHS CRAMP WITH UNGODLY PAIN—
HIS MUSCLE
TEARS FROM WITHIN HIS LEFT CALF—
HIS FEET, SOAKED FROM THE
SWAMPS HE HAS CROSSED, THE BLISTERS
SLOWLY OPEN AND RUB
THE FRICTION FROM WITHIN—AND YET—HE PUSHES ON—
HIS STOMACH AND INNER CORE ARE IN
AGANIZING PAIN—BLOOD
IS SLOWLY GETTING INTO HIS BLATTER WITHOUT
A REASON OR A
CARE—HIS HEART PUMPS AND PUSHES HARDER
AS EACH MINUTE
PASSES BY—AND YET—HE PUSHES ON—
HIS MIND FACES THE MOST CHALLENGIN DECISIONS—
THERE'S NOT
MUCH TIME FOR CHOW, FOR SLEEP, FOR REST,
OR EVEN TO STOP—AND THE
HEAT HAS NOT LET UP FROM 115° WITH HUMIDITY—
HIS FINGERS, BROKEN, JUST A
FEW, FROM THE FALLS OF FATIGUE—AND YET—HE PUSHES ON—
AND AS THE INSTRUCTOR, NEXT TO HIM, SAYS—
YOU ARE ABOUT TO BECOME A

SAFETY HAZARD IN THIS TRAINING EXCERCISE—HE REALIZES—
AS MUCH AS HE PUSHED ON—AS GREAT AS
PEOPLE THOUGHT HE'D DO
AS HARD AS HE TRAINED FOR THIS MOMENT—
HE COULD NOT PUSH ON ANY
FURTHER—EVEN AT HIS BEST—IT WASN'T ENOUGH—
HE HAD TO LET THE TEAM GO ON

*20090823*

## WHEN LIFE'S EXPERIENCES...

... DRAW YOU IN
PUSH YOU OUT
PICK YOU UP
PUSH YOU DOWN
IT SEEMS THE TEST OF LIFE WILL ALWAYS BE
THERE BUT THE CHALLENGE AND DETERMINATION TO ADHERE
IS AND WILL ALWAYS BE OUT THERE—SOME, COME UP
SHORT AND WONDER WHERE—FEW, TAKE IT TO THE TOP
WITH OUT A WORRY OR A CARE—AND OTHERS, WELL
MOST—SEE IT, WATCH IT, REFLECT ON IT AND FORGET ABOUT
IT EVER BEING THERE
AND AS THE MORNING DEW BRINGS HERE—THE SETTING
SUN TAKES TO TEAR—BECAUSE THE DAY WAS LONG BUT THE
NIGHT IS FOR THE STRONG—LIFE, LIFE IS MEANT TO... IT'S
TO... GET OUT OF IT, WHAT YOU PUT IN IT—THE GREATEST
MINDS IN THE WORLD MAY NEVER BE DISCOVERED,
MAYBE BECAUSE
THEIR TALENT IS UNDISCOVERED OR ANY NUMBER
OF REASONS BUT
WHAT I CAN TELL YOU—IS NOT TO REASON BUT TO HAVE A
PASSION—DISCOVER THE UNIMAGINABLE—BE CREATABLE,
IN-MOVABLE, AND MOST OF ALL UN-WORD-ABLE
AND WHEN YOU DO THAT—THAT'S WHEN EXPERIENCE
NEEDS NO NAME BUT UNBELIEVABLE

*8-27-2008*

## THE HOUSE OF WHICH MY FOUNDATION IS *BUILT* ON

NOT ONLY MUST YOU KNOCK—YOU MUST
ASK FOR HIS FORGIVENESS
AND ENTER—JUST LIKE THAT MOMENT IN TIME—YOU ARE A
WITNESS AND A WITNESS NOT JUST TO MIRACLES
BUT TO HIS PRESENCE—
FOR HIS SON WAS ONCE SENT AND SENTENCED—
BUT THE GLORY OF
THAT MOMENT BRINGS US TO OUR KNEES AND BEGS FOR HIS
FORGIVENESS—PLEASE, LORD, PLEASE—
LET MY PRAYER BE HEARD—
LIKE PART OF THE FLOCK—YOU ARE MY SHEPHARD—AS ONCE I
WAS LOST—AND IN TROUBLE—YOU FOUND ME AND
PROTECTED ME—
WATCHED OVER ME WITH UNCEASING LOVE—AND YOUR LOVE
CARRIES ME BACK TO BE WITH YOU—SO AS EACH DAY—I AWAKE
I THANK YOU AND PRAISE YOU—AMEN—BUT IT CAN'T STOP
WITH JUST THE PRAYER—
BECAUSE LIKE ALL MEN—WE ARE DOOMED TO SIN—
BUT YOU NOTICE—
THE BIBLE—STILL IN MY HAND—HIS WORDS ARE WHAT I TAKE
AND INTERPRIT INTO MY OWN LIFE—EVEN MY FAMILY, KIDS,
AND WIFE—BECAUSE TOGETHER WE PUT OUR LOVE AND TRUST
IN YOU UNTIL THE END OF TIME—
NOW OF COURSE THE GROUND
WILL SHAKE AND TRY TO BREAK OUR HOUSE—BUT WITH YOU AS
OUR FOUNDATION—THERE IS NO WORRY—
LET ME SAY IT AGAIN AND LISTEN CLOSELY—THERE IS
NO WORRY—

*MARCH 30$^{TH}$ 2008*

## HIS NOISE

LORD, YOUR MY REASON—FOR LIVIN—
AND MY FREEDOM IS FOUND—
NOT IN INDIANA OR WISCONSIN—BUT MARYLAND—
SO MANY FRIENDS
ARE SET ACROSS A WIDE BRAND—BUT HOPEFULLY I REACH
EVERY AND ALL TOWNS AND HOMELANDS.
JUST ONE MAN COULDN'T
HAVE DONE WHAT HE DID—
BUT HIS FAITHFULNESS HAVE LET THE
YOUTH BE PUT OUT AND DISTRIBUTED—
I'M SO TIRED AND WOREN
OUT, BUT YOUR PRAYERS AND THOUGHTS
HAVE MADE ME WANNA
SHOUT—LETS JUST THANK THE LORD THAT
OUR DREAMS BE BROUGHT
ABOUT—FOR THE FUTURE DEPENDS—NO MATTER
THE BENDS OR TURNS
IN THE ROAD AHEAD—BECAUSE MY HEART IS SET TO LIVE THIS
ROAD AHEAD—WHETHER IT'S BROKEN
OR STRAIGHT AHEAD—THIS
PAVED AND OUTTA NO RESPECT—MY BODY
TEARS APART—BUT STILL
REMAINS—MY UNCULTURED AND BLESSED HEAD.
SO HERE I LEAVE
A TRAIL—AND LET ALL WHO BELIEVE—TREAD AND NEVER STOP
OR FAIL—SO BOX ME UP AND PUT ME IN THE MAIL—BUT DON'T
DROP, FOR THE FRAGILNESS—IF DROPPED—
WILL FALL AS HARD AS
HAIL. IT SEEMS TO ASK—IF HEAVEN—THEN HELL?
BUT MY SINS HE CAN ALREADY—SEE AND TELL—AND NOW
MY TALE OF DREAMS BEGINS TO FOLLOW NO TRAIL—BUT
STAYS AS STEADY AS A RAIL, BUT THIS IS MY DEAL—BUT
NOT A GAME—FOR MY FAME—IS GIVEN ALL TO FEEL

HIS WORD AND LET HIM BEGIN TO HEAL—IT'S AMAZING—
WHEN HE WAS HERE—BECAUSE NOTHING
TO FEAR—BUT AROUND
MY NECK—I CARRY THE CROSS OF A TEAR—THAT ONLY
THE ONES WHO TRULY FEEL—IT DOESN'T MATTER WHAT
THEY WEAR—OR HOW THEY LIVE—FOR IF NO DIFFERENCE—
HIS LIGHT WOULD BE SMALLER THAN A SILENCE.

*JULY 17$^{TH}$ 2005*

## THIS LIFE

THEY CALL THIS WORK CAMP—LETS—JUST
HOPE WE DON'T PASS THE OFF RAMP—AND
SO THEY SAY IT'S GONNA BE A DAMP AND WET
ONE—BUT THIS DRIVE IS KILLIN ME—MORE ROAD
AND NEVER DONE, SO EVERY DOLLAR AND CENT—WE
PUT INTO OUR TRIP OF FUN—BUT THEY SEEM
TO THINK WERE THE GOD SENT—AND SO HERE WE
PRAISE AND PREACH ABOUT THE ALMIGHTY-LORD, EVEN
IN ACCIDENT—SO IF WE HAVE TO SLEEP ON COLD
TILE OR EVEN CONCRET—BUT THE JOB WE CAME FOR
AND NOW TOWARDS THE END—EVERYONE KNOWS WHAT
WAS MEANT—NEVER BEND THE RULES TO MEND—
US THE SO CALLED—NEW TREND—TOGETHER—BUT
AS THE ROAD GETS FURTHER—OUR LOVE FOR
ONE ANOTHER GETS CONSIDERED—NEVER COLD, BUT
ALWAYS STRONGER, WE'VE ALL BEEN BOLD THROUGH
EVEN THE DARKEST OF ALL OUR MOMENTS—BY
FAITH AND TRUST. IN OUR 'BAD NEWS' MOMENTS,
LOVE AND CARE. IN OUR 'HURTFUL' MOMENTS, BUT
NOTHING COULD PREPARE US FOR WHAT THIS
COUNTRY AND HOMELAND, COULD MAKE INTO SOME OF OUR
GREATEST ACCOMPLISHMENTS. EVEN HERE IN MARYLAND—
BUT THIS LIFE THAT'S LIVED ISN'T IN A FAIRYTALE
AND A DREAM LAND. BUT THE WORD OF GOD CAN
NEVER FAIL—FOR IT'S ALL OF US IN HERE RIGHT
NOW, THAT START OUT—SOME EVEN IN A HALLOW, BUT
LEAVE THE TRAIL—AND EVEN MORE REDEEM AND FOLLOW.—
WE NEVER STOP, FORGET, OR EVEN DITCH—BUT LIKE
MY BRO T-LO—HE EVEN GOT ME—'JOE'

CLICKED AND HITCHED. SO THE GOOD LORD CAN
USE ME TO GET THE WORD OUT AND DISTRIPUTED.
SO AS THE LIGHT HE GAVE US IS BURNIN'—
WE WILL BE OUT HERE FIGHTIN', WORKIN', AND HELPIN—
EVERY OTHER HUMAN AND PERSON. AND AS THE SPEELIN'—
ROAD COMES TO A WINDIN' AND A STOPIN'—BUT AS
THE READIN'—I'M STOPPIN'—FOR THE PREACHIN' I'M
GONNA PUT ALL THIS LOVE INTO ACTION, AND LET
US NEVER LOSE THE THOUGHT TO KEEP PRAYIN.
BUT TONIGHT THE THANKS IS TO THE PARENTS—
AND HOW THEY GOT THEIR KIDS HERE—FOR THE
FUTURE DEPENDS AND IS IN THEIR HANDS

*JULY 5${}^{TH}$ 2005*

## AGAIN

IF I'D SPENT A LOT MORE TIME WITH MY FAMILY /
WHEN THEY NEEDED ME. /
IF I'D LIVED THAT LIFE OF A CHRISTIAN, /
I'D PROBABLY NOT HAVE SO MANY
SCARS AND STUPID SUPERSTITIONS. /
BUT AS I GREW UP, /
I CONSIDERED MYSELF A LOW BROW, /
AN UNCULTURED; AND I WISH I KNEW
THEN WHAT I KNOW NOW, /
IN MY DAYS OF GROWING UP, /
IT WAS ALWAYS TO PROSPER. /
IT NEVER MATTERED WHAT THEIR ATTITUDE WAS—/ LIKE
OR HOW THEY GAVE OFF EVEN A GESTURE. / IT'S LIKE MY LIFE
IS A MASSACRE . . . /ALWAYS BURNING UP WITH
A FEVER. / WALKING
INTO ROOMS, I ALWAYS FEEL LIKE THE INTRUDER. / THIS LIFE WE
LIVE WAS AND IS PREFABRICATED,—JUST LIVED IN SECTIONS. /
WITH NO ONE TO TURN TO UNLESS YOU'RE A SUCCESS IN ALL
YOUR MISSIONS. / AM I EVEN ABLE? / I'M UNPREDICTABLE, /
UNSTABLE, /
AND UNFAVORABLE. / NOW I'M NOT EVEN WORTHY
OF BEING CONSIDERED
PART OF THE FAMILY. / I DON'T KNOW. MAYBE IF YOU SEE WHAT
I SEE, / YOU'D UNDERSTAND, / BUT—
PEOPLE SAY QUIT IMPOSING, /
JUST LIVE AND PROTECT YOUR HOMELAND / AND STOP
PROMISING

*FEB 15<sup>TH</sup> 2005*

## YOUR CHILDRENS PLAN

A KIDS LIFE IS A GIFT—
BUT ONCE THEY GROW—
HOW OFTEN WE GET CAUGHT IN THE DRIFT—
AND SOMETIMES FORGET THAT WITH GOD WE HAVE A
TOMORROW—
AND THAT HE IS OUR FOUNDATION—
STRONG AND FIRM—
BECAUSE HE HAS A MUCH GREATER DESTINATION—
WITH A PROMISE IN RETURN—
THAT AFTER MY CHILDREN LIVE THEIR LIFE BY
THE STANDARDS I SET
THE YOUTH WILL BE AT 'GET READY, SET . . .'—
BUT YOU AS THE PARENTS HAVE TO LET GO AND BET—
THAT YOUR KIDS LIFE, DON'T WORRY, THEY'LL
MAKE THE MOST OF IT—
AND DON'T THINK OF HOW HARD IT'S GOING TO GET—
BUT RATHER PRAY—THAT THEY MAKE THE MOST OF IT—

*SEPT. 9<sup>TH</sup> 2006*

## I HOPED THEY'D SAY I MADE A DIFFERENCE

ALL THE MISTAKES I'VE MADE
IN LIFE, MY MOMS FOUND OUT
ABOUT AND PROFESSED TO ADDRESS THAT
SHE'S JADED AND WORN-OUT, BUT SHE'S
MY LOOK-OUT, AND SHE'S INFESTED WITH
THE LOW-DOWN-THE WHOLE TRUTH, EVERY
FACT, AND THAT SHE'LL LOVE ME, THROUGH
ALL THAT GOES DOWN
AND THROUGH ALL I ATTACK. MOM NEVER
HELD ME BACK OR PLACED CHAINS,
BUT OPENED THE GATES, AND SAID
HANG ON TO THE REIGNS. SO NOW
THE START OF A FURIOUS SERMON
THAT WITHOUT DENIAL,
IS ENDIN AND BENDIN'
MY THOUGHTS I WAS SEEIN-BELIVIN'—
AND LIVE-IN'. IS MY REVALATION COMING
TO A REVOLUTION THAT ONLY THE
CHOSEN WITH THE MARKS, AND SCARS, CAN GIVE
THE PREDICTION OF WHICH WAY WE NEED TO
BE GO-IN, NO RUNNIN' AND HIDDIN,
FROM ALL THE CONFUSION, BUT AS THEY ALL DEFY
ME AND MY MEANIN'—IT'S THEM I REQUEST TO BE SLIDIN'
INTO THIS FIRE I'M BURNIN'

*JUNE 28TH 2006*

# DISTRESS

DISTRESS—IN THE LOWEST
CIPHER IS TAKEN
TO BRING ABOUT THE IMAGINED
CHARACTER THAT THE MOROSE
AND BOASTFULL PERSON WOULD
CHANGE AND STRIVE TO
COMPETE AGAINST. BUT JUST
TO EMULATE THE POSSIBILITY
THAT THERE MIGHT BE AN
OPPURTUNITY TO JOIN THE
CURVED PLANE THAT BELONGS
TO THE FERMENTED AND PERPETUAL
DARKNESS THAT POINTS TO
THE FLEECY JOURNEY THAT
COURTS ANYTHING THAT
MEASURES TO SAY THAT THEY
BELONG TO THIS PRIVATE
APERTURE THAT'S UNCONTAINABLE
IN IT'S EXCESSIVE MATTER OF
CONDUCT TO THOSE PRODUCED
FROM THE CHURCH WHOSE PROTESTANT
DISSENTER IS DIPLOMATIC IN
HIS STRUGGLE OF POLISHING THE PRACTICE
OF ONE DAY GATHERING
AND AWARDING THOSE WHO
COMPOSED A SPIRITUAL FEELING
THAT ASSOCIATED THE INFLUENCE
OF MAKING A SUMPTUOUS
CONCEPTION THAT'S FRIGID
AND DIFFICULT FOR EVEN
THE IMPAIRED HUNTSMEN WHO'S
URGE TO ACT WITH MORE
CELERITY, SO THAT THE
VIEW OF PERFECTION SEEMS
POSSIBLE, BUT WHAT
A DISSEMBLER DOES—
IS NOT TO BE MIRRORED—

NOR RE-NOUNED, BECAUSE HE'LL
BETAKE THE REMAINDER
OF YOUR REPUTATION AND
WITHDRAW BEFORE YOU
CAN COLLECT YOUR RENDER
AND SO HE DEPENDS ON THOSE
WHO RETAIN A NON-DELIGERENT
ECHO—BECAUSE WITH THEM HE'S GOT A CONNECTION, BUT
WHEN YOU UNDERESTIMATE JOE—YOU FORGOT
TO MENTION—THE
STORY AND LAYOUT—OF WHERE HE MOUNTS
BECAUSE YOU'RE CORRUPTED
BY THE ORDER OF FRAMES THAT ACT IN MANY AMOUNTS—SO
YOUR CONFIDENCE IS CREDITED TO THE PEOPLE
WHO MAKE IT ALL COUNT

*JULY 2ND 2006*

## WHAT'S NEXT

AFTER GOOD OF THE ORDER
IT SEEMS THE STORM MOVES IN
AND ALL YOU CAN HEAR IS THE THUNDER—
BUT WHEN YOU'RE LOCKED IN A PIN—
YOU'LL DO ANYTHING TO TAKE COVER—
BECAUSE IN PRISON YOU'LL DO ANYTHING
TO BE THE GUARD RATHER THAN THE PRISONER—
SO EVENTUALLY WE PROTEST AND TAKE OVER—
AND FINALLY GIVE BACK TO THE COMMUNITY
THAT WE ONCE WISHED FOR DISASTER—
AND NOW THERE'S A NEW ROAD TO UNCOVER—
AND WE'RE NO LONGER—THE PEOPLE YOU NEVER
WANTED TO SEE—BUT RATHER THE TEACHER
THAT MAKES YOU BECOME ALL YOU CAN BE—
SO ARE MERCY—IS YOUR GRACE—BECAUSE WHEN
YOU LOOK AT OUR PAST IN OUR FACE—YOU
SEE MORE THAN THE AVERAGE—WE'RE NOT
A DISCRACE, BUT A MIRROR IMAGE OF
WHAT THEY DON'T WANT TO BECOME BECAUSE
OF THE STORIES WE TELL—SO LET ME HEAR
YOU SCREAM AND YELL—FOR NOW'S THE
TIME TO SHOW THEM IT'S ALL UP FOR SALE—

*AUG 2$^{ND}$ 2007*

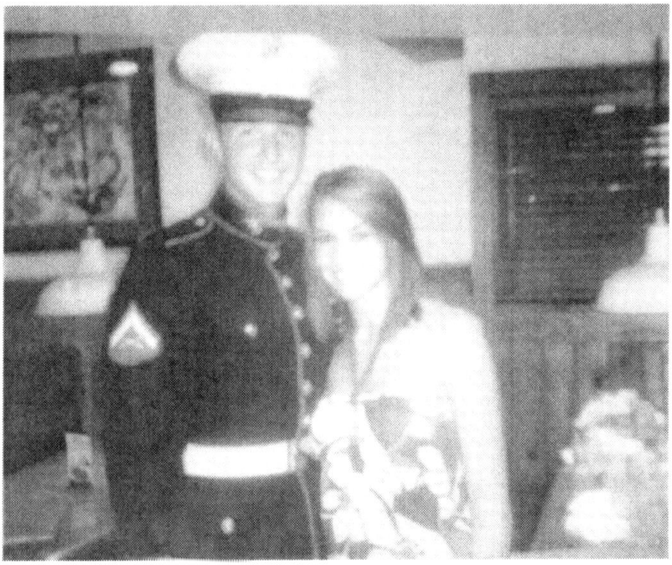

## THE STITCHING STARE

MY MIRROR—
THE GUY IN IT IS AS USELESS AS HIS GLARE—
BECAUSE THIS NIGHTMARE—
I CAN'T BEAR—
I CAN'T SEE, CAN'T BREATH—AS IF THERE'S NO MORE AIR—
SO NOW ONE'S I HELD CLOSE—NOW ME THEY FEAR—
NO REASON, NO CARE—
SO I'LL PUT AN END TO THIS NIGHTMARE—
NOW AT HELLS GATES, THE DEMONS CHEER—
WHILE GOD SITS AND OPENS HIS MOUTH ONLY TO SWEAR—
AND HOW WRONG I WAS TO DREAM OF BEING ONE
OF HIS PERFECT AND RARE—
SO WHAT'S LEFT TO DO, EXCEPT ATTEMPT THIS DARE—
I'VE GOT MY GEAR—
BUT WHETHER I USE IT OR NOT, I NO LONGER CARE—

*SEPT. 9<sup>TH</sup> 2006*

## WAR / ART / TRAIN / INSIDE / WARTRAINSIDE

WHETHER THE EVENTS UNFOLDED
NEAR OR ABROAD—IT WAS TO HAPPEN
WITH NO OBJECTION—BUT WHEN
THE VOICES OF CHILDREN ARE
NO LONGER POISED IN A NATION—
EVERYONE MUST QUESTION THIS
SITUATION THAT THEY'RE CREATIN'
BUT WHEN YOU'RE ONE LESS 2 SHORT
OF AN OPTION'—YOUR LAST THOUGHT OF
A CONDITION IS NOW THE LIFE THAT
YOU WOULDN'T WANT TO BE LIVIN'—NOW SOME SAY
THE IMPLEMENTATION' OF HIS PLAN—IS
JUST A WARRED OFF FACTION—BUT
TO THOSE WHO LISTENED TO THE WORDS
WRITTEN IN TRANSACTION—THEY'D TELL YOU—
THAT HIS RESTORATION' WAS MORE EMPOWERED
THAN ANY OTHER PROCREATION'

*MAY 10<sup>TH</sup> 2009*

## HOME IS NOT REALLY A PLACE AT ALL

AN INTERROGATION
IS YOUR IMAGINATION
OF YOUR IMAGE OF WHAT'S
IMAGINABLE WHEN YOU'RE CAPABLE
OF DESTRUCTING THE
UNBUILDABLE BY
FABLE STORYTELLERS
WHO GATHERED TO
ARTICLE THE UNBELIEVEABLE—
BUT FOR THE UNSTOPPABLE
THEY WERE ABLE TO MAKE
MARKETABLE AND AVAILABLE—
SO TO ALL OTHERS THAT ARE
DISAGREEABLE BECAUSE OF THE HYPOTHETICAL
THINKERS WHO'VE SHOWN
TO ALL—THE UNPREDICTABLE
THAT'S SAID TO BE UNCHANGEABLE
AND FOREVER WORKABLE BECAUSE
WHEN FIRST LAID OUT ON THE TABLE
IT WAS REASONABLE, BUT DEBATABLE
WITH MANY QUESTIONS LIKE IS IT CONTROLLABLE
AND WILL THEY EVER
BECOME SO DESIRABLE
TO FIND AN ANSWER
FOR THEIR SURVIVAL—
SO WE NEED YOU TO
VERIFY THE WAY
THAT THIS IS UNMISTAKEABLE
AND UNBREAKABLE

*NOV 1ST 2008*

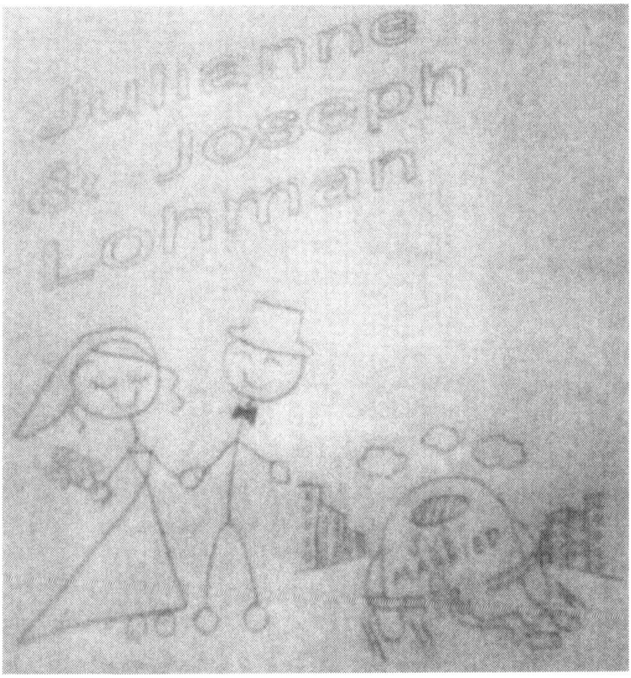
Julienne
& Joseph
Lohman

## IS IT INSPIRATION

THE DARKEST MOTION—
IS CAPABLE OF CHANGIN—
ANY FORCE THAT'S
PROJECTIN' AN INTERACTION,
INDICATION', OR CONSCIOUS
DECISION—OF WHAT'S GOING
TO BE THEIR DECISION—SO
AT ONE POINT IN POSITION—
TO STEP BACK AND LOOK
AT THIS EQUATION THAT ONE
IS CREATIN'—IS A MISTAKE
WORTH TRYIN', TAKEN, OR FAILIN'—

*JUNE 8$^{TH}$ 2008*

## THE LIMITS OF IMAGE

THE BOUNDARIES WE ALL ENCOUNTER—
SEEM TO HAUNT US INTO OUR FUTURE PAST FOREVER—
AND AS OUR MEMORIES STAND LONG AFTER—
OUR KIDS WILL BE HERE TO CARRY ON
LIFE FOR THE BETTER—
BUT THE MISTAKES WE MAKE WILL FOREVER
BE NEXT TO US LIKE THE GHOSTS WHO HAUNT
US INTO OUR FUTURE PRESENT DISASTER—
NO FUTURE TELLERS CAN GIVE YOU THE OUTCOME
OF THE NIGHT WHICH IS TO COME
SOONER THAN LONG AFTER—BUT AS EACH PASSING DAY—
HALLOWEEN NIGHT IS TO BE GETTING CLOSER
AND COLDER—SO AS THE WIND STIRS—THE
LEAVES IN THE TREES—THERE'S A SUDDEN CRACK OF
THUNDER—WHICH SCARES ALL FROM THE STREETS AND
BACK INTO THEIR SO CALLED HOMES OF COMFORT—
BUT AS THE RAIN POURS DOWN OVER THE KIDS,
HIDDEN, NOT TO
DISCOVERED—THE POWER TO WHICH RUNS THE
SHELTER—IS GONE FOREVER—AND
ALL YOU CAN HEAR—ARE THEIR HEARTS BEATING FASTER AND
FASTER

*OCT 31$^{ST}$ 2008*

## A PRIMITIVE GIVING

IT SEEMS THE LIFE THAT WE HAVE BEEN
LIVING—IS MADE UP OF 3 DIFFERENT
PARTS, TO WHICH BE FITTING—FIRST,
IS THE FAMOUS, POWERFUL, AND RICH
*PERSON*—TO WHOM WE ALL WOULD
RATHER NOT BE KNOWING—SECOND, IS THE
MEDIOCRE, AVERAGE 9-5,
WHO WOULD GIVE ANYTHING—
NOT TO BE LOOKED AT AS THE *PERSON*
WHO NEVER TRUSTED THE WORD THAT HE HAD
PUT IN WRITING—AND LASTLY, IS A
FIGMENT OF EVERYONE'S' BLINDNESS—TO
WHICH IS DIS-HEARTENING, BUT WHEN
LOOKED AT THROUGH OPEN EYES—IT CAN
CHANGE THE WAY ALL THREE ARE SEEING—
BECAUSE WHEN TEARS ARE FALLING,—
EMOTIONS ARE CHANGING—AND HEARTS
ARE OPENING AND CONTRIBUTING—TO THEIR
ONCE LOST SELF IMAGING—SO DO
WHAT'S RIGHT—BEFORE THEIR END
IS ANOTHERS BEGINNING—

*JAN 18$^{TH}$ 2009*

## J. O. Y.

WHAT DO YOU SAY TO
THE GIRL THAT MAKES YOU
FEEL LIKE AS IF YOUR
ON TOP OF THE WORLD.
SOMEHOW I DON'T THINK
ANY AMOUNT OF WORDS
COULD EXPRESS HOW HER
BEAUTY CONTAINS ME AND
CAPTURES AND CULTIVATES
ME. BUT FINALLY FOR ONCE IN
MY LIFE I HAVE FOUND THE REASON
I HAVE ASKED *G*OD SO MANY TIMES FOR!
THIS REASON IS NOT JUST A REASON TO
SURVIVE BUT TO ACTUALLY LIVE LIFE FOR
THE MOMENT—BECAUSE WHEN I'M IN HER PRESENCE—
TIME, IS NO LONGER AN INTEREST, AND FOR
EVERYDAY THAT SHE SMILES AND SAYS THAT SHE'S
NOT THE ANGEL THAT I SEE—IT ONLY MAKES
ME SMILE AND KEEP RIGHT ON THINKING THAT—

*NOV 30<sup>TH</sup> 2007*

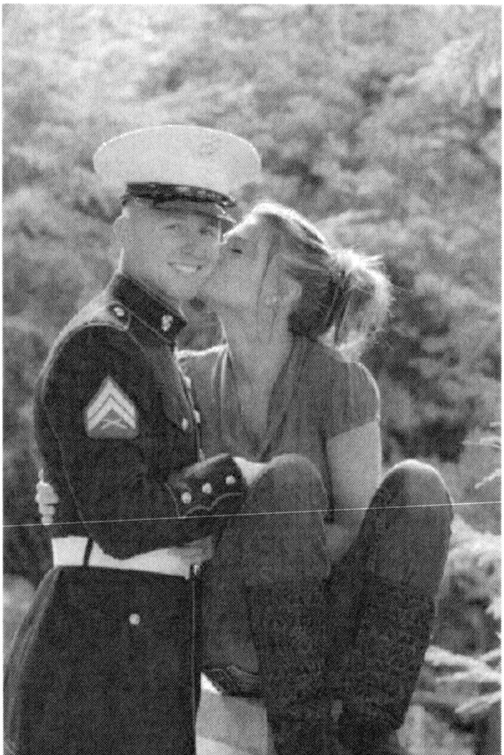

## JUST A SMILE

TO SAY THAT HER SMILE IS THAT OF AN ANGEL—WOULDN'T BE ENOUGH. TO SAY THAT HER EYES ARE LIKE GEMS THAT GOD HAD PLACED HIMSELF—WOULDN'T BE ENOUGH. AND TO SAY THAT I FORGOT COMPLICATED, DIFFICULT, AND CONFUSING . . . WELL THOSE ARE ALL THE MORE REASONS—I WANT TO GET TO KNOW HER. BECAUSE I KNOW WE'RE NOT PERFECT BUT AFTER SECOND BY SECOND, MIN BY MIN, HOUR BY HOUR, DAY BY DAY, AND YEAR BY YEAR—WE MAY COME TO FIND THAT WE'RE PERFECT FOR EACH OTHER—COURSE, TIMES WILL BE TOUGH AND THE MOMENTS WE SHARE WILL BE GREAT—AND MAYBE SOMEDAY WHEN WERE OLD AND SITTING TOGETHER—WE CAN SAY—JUST THINK OF WHAT WE COULD HAVE LOST IF WE HADN'T TAKEN THIS CHANCE; OUR KIDS, GRANDKIDS, MEMORIES, AND OF COURSE MY PERSONAL FAVORITE—GETTING TO KNOW MY BEST FRIEND

*NOV 9TH 2007*

## A Farmers Hardship

The day is soft, my lips are moist
The touch of a woman, still lingers on my skin
The air of a fresh breeze
presses up against
The flag of this nation as it
hangs upon a tall podem
as it stretches o so far
My lip pressed and formed with a dip
The taste of far bitter shit
and I wettin the ground
with the juices of my spit
But as the day's sun sets on
there is still lots of work to which must be done
I gather my thoughts under this oak
After each mornin' . . . I put on each boot
And when the day's end draws out
I will be with my family throughout this drought

*NOV 29TH 2009*

## silence in my room

As I sit and ponder in the vast sky
of my closed eyes
My imagination opens vigorously
I try to resist nature's side that's not so pretty
For i have just come home, from war
with another country
One of my friends did not, and left
me responsible for his family
And all I can do is slautch on
my elbows with one of my hands holding my head
Just thinkin and cryin
My thoughts are just an illusion
an illustration . . . Of my friend . . .
who i held in my arms, as he
talked about his wife and kids
I sat there; in my boots
my brown filthy cammies, my protective gear
and my gun and the fact remains
we lost one

*OCT 15<sup>TH</sup> 2009*

## my lady

she is that of an angel
sent from the heavens
she has the eyes of the lords two brightest stars
there is not a day that passes that i am not hers
her heart is strong
it has more love than i could ever dream of
she is my sunrise and my sunset
her smile is what captures and cultivates me
she is a girl that is far more better
than any dream i could ever imagine
she is what keeps me going
when the going gets tough
she is the touch that cannot be expressed
because with her hand in mine
we will be together through all of time
she has a voice that needs no rhyme
it is such a soft and delicate feature
which is one of many to which she calls mine
And her name is Julianne
the love of my life and soon to be my wife.
i love you 8.7.09


*JAN 31ST 2010*

## Julianne & Joseph

8-7-09
*Forever*
*Our Sea Shells*

*Both* have their own designs, their own
curves and grooves, each has a certain
pattern and color about them, and each
of them were from 2 different parts in
the world, they have a round top which
leaves alot of empty space underneath them.
But in that space, it's not just air or water,
it contains its history, it holds its secrets,
and each shell protects it's keeper. And
when listened closely with it to our ear you
can hear it tell its story.
Baby you are my shell and i am
yours! I love your secrets, your curves
and grooves, i' love your story, your history, the good times
and the bad because i am here for you and i will
always protect you and love you
xoxo joey


*March 2ⁿᵈ 2010*

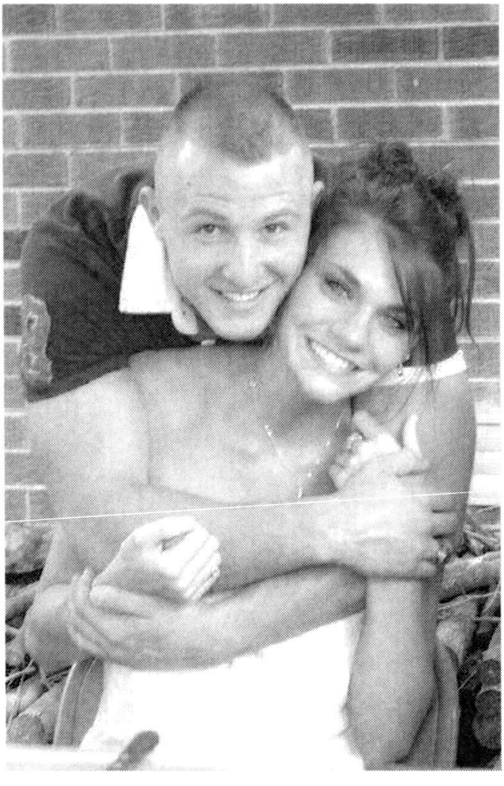